PRACTICAL REASONING

How the experience of the Humanities can help train doctors

Ronald Schleifer

PRAGMATICS OF ART

University of Canberra

Centre for Creative and Cultural Research

Series editor: Distinguished Professor Jen Webb

1 Pierre Bourdieu, *Thinking about Art – at Art School* Translated by Michael Grenfell. Edited by Scott Brook.

2 Ronald Schleifer, *Practical Reasoning: How the experience of the Humanities can help train doctors*. Edited with an introduction by Jen Crawford.

PRACTICAL REASONING

How the experience of the Humanities can help train doctors

Ronald Schleifer

Introduction by Jen Crawford

PRAGMATICS OF ART 2

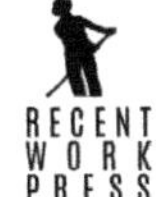

University of Canberra
Centre for Creative and Cultural Research

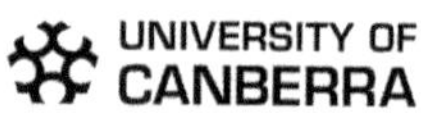

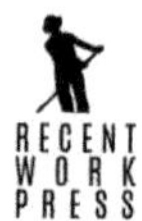

First published in 2017 by
Centre for Creative and Cultural Research, with Recent Work Press
Faculty of Arts and Design, University of Canberra, ACT 2601
Australia

ISBN: 978-0-64808-788-5 (paperback)

Publication editor: Jen Crawford
Publication design and layout: Caren Florance

Cover: image by Darksair Sun, after Jerry Spagnoli:
https://www.flickr.com/photos/corsair/8912611067/

Contents

vii *Series Introduction*

Jen Webb

Distinguished Professor, University of Canberra
Director, Centre for Creative and Cultural Research
General Editor, The Pragmatics of Art

1 *Introduction: Practical Reasoning and the Pragmatics of Art*

Jen Crawford

Assistant Professor,
Centre for Creative and Cultural Research
Faculty of Arts & Design
University of Canberra

13 A Listing of Work in Medical Humanities by Ronald Schleifer

17 *Practical Reasoning: How the Experience of the Humanities can Help Train Doctors*

Ronald Schleifer

George Lynn Cross Research Professor
Adjunct Professor in Medicine
Department of English
University of Oklahoma

57 Bibliography

Series Introduction

The Centre for Creative and Cultural Research (CCCR) within the Faculty of Arts and Design at the University of Canberra focuses on applied research into creative practice. Staff, research students, adjuncts and visitors work on key challenges within the creative field and the cultural sector. The focus of our work is to conduct imaginative and practical experiments at the intersection of creative writing, digital technology and contemporary heritage practice. Many of the CCCR's members are creative practitioners who produce not only traditional scholarly outputs, but also creative publications and performances, exhibitions and exhibition design, and professional inputs to cultural and community institutions. Poetry, material poetics, narrative practices and exhibition practices are at the heart of our research activity. In addition, the CCCR facilitates a series of intensive creative workshops with people suffering from trauma and related issues, and is developing knowledge and skills about the relationship between art practice, creative thinking, and resilience.

This series, The Pragmatics of Art, aims to model and disseminate the combination of practical and intellectual research that guides the work of our Centre, and to provide thoughtful contributions from a wide variety of sources to artistic and intellectual projects that both derive from and serve larger communities. In a way, the series represents a working laboratory for students, artists, and scholars interested in learning to integrate the arts and skills of artistic knowledges and design into other branches of practical and intellectual work in our society.

Distinguished Professor Jen Webb

Director,
Centre for Creative and Cultural Research
University of Canberra

General Editor,
The Pragmatics of Art

Practical Reasoning and the Pragmatics of Art

Jen Crawford

It is my pleasure to introduce the essay that follows by Professor Ronald Schleifer, the George Lynn Cross Distinguished Research Professor of English and also Adjunct Professor in Medicine at the University of Oklahoma. As Professor Schleifer notes in the essay, he has taught and worked with members of the Faculty of Medicine, medical students, and undergraduate pre-med students at the University of Oklahoma for more than twenty years. He has also served as the Chair of the Publications Committee of the Society for Literature, Science, and the Arts, where he has promoted the medical humanities in the United States for many years. In addition, he has published widely in cultural modernism, semiotics, and narrative theory, areas that inform his long-term project, outlined in this volume, of developing practical skills in relation to literature, music, and the arts that can serve physicians, medical students, and medical faculties. I am appending to this introduction a list of his work in the medical humanities spanning the last seventeen years, conducted both in print and in person. As well as helping to introduce him to you as an author and to document one branch of his prolific research career, this will serve to indicate the expansive growth of the medical humanities in recent years, both in the US and internationally, as it is increasingly integrated into the training of physicians and healthcare workers.

There is a long history of connections between literature, the arts, and medicine. From the very beginning of formal training in healthcare and medicine this has been so. In ancient Greece, Hippocrates suggested that medicine was both a science and an art, and, as Schleifer notes in his essay in this volume, Aristotle – whose father was a physician – describes his concept of *phronesis*, or 'practical reasoning,' in *The Nicomachean Ethics* with the work of physicians as his chief example. In terms of literature, many great writers beginning in the eighteenth century – Oliver Goldsmith, Tobias Smollett, John Keats, Anton Chekhov, Arthur Conan Doyle, W. H. Auden, Ernest Hemingway, and many more – were physicians, healthcare workers, or closely related to physicians. Over the past two decades many, if not most, medical colleges in the United States have instituted courses – often mandatory – in the medical humanities for their students, and in the United Kingdom most undergraduate medical programs offer either mandatory or optional courses in one or more humanities subjects at some point in the degree.

The medical humanities can be defined as interdisciplinary studies and teaching that draw upon the creative and intellectual work of disciplines outside of biomedicine to contribute to the education of physicians and healthcare workers.

These disciplines include social sciences such as anthropology, cultural studies, sociology, and the arts (poetry, fiction and creative non-fiction, the visual and plastic arts, music). In the essay that follows, Schleifer argues vigorously that 'the humanities can be understood as being as systematically rigorous as the nomological (or "law-like") sciences that have been the mainstay of training in medical schools since the beginnings of formal medical education at the beginning of the twentieth century... [which] has recently come to be called "evidence-based medicine."'

With this noted, it's well worth considering the medical humanities as but one example of the kind of discipline-expanding work that the humanities make possible in many domains. Schleifer makes the case that the humanities train us in systematic attention to experience – and in particular, attention to linguistic and narrative knowledge – and he shows how this kind of attention can change the fundamental quality and outcome of interactions in the domain of medicine. In the Centre for Creative and Cultural Research, our work is founded in this kind of systematic attention, its development in research, and the application of that research within a broad range of contexts including in healthcare, heritage conservation, design, media, cultural policy and community development. Precisely because we understand, on the basis of both research and lived experience, the capacity of narrative work to transform the organization and outcomes of social action in these contexts, there is a focus throughout CCCR's activity on how narrative shapes and interprets the world.

Discussions of the social functions of the humanities are not without their tensions. Scholars and practitioners of the humanities and particularly the arts are well accustomed to having to argue for the independent value of their work. The disciplinary autonomy of creative practitioners (even if one follows Adorno in understanding art's social autonomy to be both necessary and illusory) helps to secure agency and integrity in their practitioners' responses to social materials and conditions. Accordingly, practice-based research, which understands the making of creative works as generating knowledge as well as artefacts, is alongside textual and social research, core to the CCCR's activities. The activity of the CCCR's International Poetry Studies Institute in developing and disseminating new poetry works is one fine example.

Yet we also know through practical experience that creative autonomy can continue to thrive in interdisciplinary environments. One salient current example of this is the Defence ARRTS Project ('Arts for Recovery, Resilience, Teamwork, and Skills,' part of our Centre's developing focus on Arts and Trauma) which offers training for injured returning armed forces personnel. In the ARRTS program, participants are themselves the makers of texts (written stories, poems, visual artworks or performances), trained by writers and artists who work alongside healthcare practitioners and researchers to promote and assess the recovery value of the program. The interdisciplinary nature of the team allows the outcomes to be evaluated, contributing to research knowledge on the effects of this kind of intervention, the very pragmatics of art. Thus far, the outcomes suggest this training has significant effects on numerous measures of recovery, bolstering participants' self-reported self esteem, social functioning, physical functioning and positive affect, while reducing their psychological distress, insomnia, and post-traumatic stress. This is valuable information that contributes to 'results-based' evidence of the wellbeing effects promoted and sustained in an arts program.

For the participants, though, it is often the 'free-play' nature of their immersion in the arts – offering the freedom to participate without the need to produce defined outcomes – that helps to produce its wellbeing effects. This is not to suggest that creative work somehow exists outside the kinds of schemas of meaning that Schleifer discusses in the essay to follow. Rather, it is to suggest that, as we know from many years of teaching creative writing, creative practice itself (like and often alongside the practices of reading and analysis) allows the practitioner to become intimate with such schemas – schemas that, as readers of literary narrative experience, don't constrain the many possibilities of a text, but rather hold it in meaningful relationship to their experience of other narratives, other artefacts of meaning – the texts that exist before, around and even as traces within the text at hand. This is the value of Schleifer's emphasis on the provisional nature of cognitive and cultural schemas. In making, just as in reading, we awaken our attention to aspects of experience that might otherwise go unnoticed. We also train our attention to make this kind of noticing habitual. This is what he means by 'discipline' in this essay and what we mean by the 'pragmatics' of art at the Centre for Creative and Cultural Research here at the University of Canberra: the development of habitual attention and skills of understanding and action that allow us to contribute to the communities in which we live and work through the kind of *phronesis* or 'practical reasoning' that such skills and attention allow and promote.

Schleifer is not exactly describing 'free play' in the patient-physician encounters that are narrated by his colleague, Dr Jerry Vannatta in the essay that follows. Still, he and Dr Vannatta advocate in their book, *The Chief Concern of Medicine*, that the protocols of the clinical interview should allow for the possibility of negotiating the meaning of 'health,' and such negotiation requires the acknowledgment of the active participation – the active agency – of the patient. The story that Dr Vannatta recounts of a patient who had suffered childhood abuse from her father suggests both the promise and the risk that is always part of encounters with illness, both for the patient and the caregiver. To my ear, the narrative Dr Vannatta presents suggests that the young woman patient is a partner in her own rescue, that her ability to give voice to her history – even at the prompting of her physician – is at least in part an act of chosen self-advocacy. Nevertheless, neither Vannatta's presentation of the story nor Schleifer's discussion of it takes into account the darker side of her history: not only the fact that people are changed by trauma and they don't readily change back, but also *practical* problems of the complexities of treatment, the small expectations of the availability of appropriate psychotherapeutic treatment for anyone but the rich, the systemic dimunition of women in society. I think different readers will have very different experiences in reading this scene: pleasure that the doctor has figured out the source of his patient's illness and has done the right thing versus discomfort and distress at the perpetuation of the conditions of trauma even in a moment which promises healing. To these latter readers, the interns' dismissal and miscategorisation of this young woman's condition would probably create more long-term harm but have less acute traumatic energy than the clinical moment with Dr Vannatta, which promises so much and in which, therefore, so much is at stake. The 'practical reasoning' that Schleifer discusses is not always an easy science; it calls upon the difficulties and discomfort of thoughtful self- and social-reflection that he talks about and, as in my reflection on this scene, calls upon his readers to pursue.

To end this Introduction, I want to offer the example of a particular poem to elucidate the practical reasoning that is engaged in both its making and its reading in a context that is less traumatically charged than those of patients and caretakers faced with terrible illness in Dr Vannatta's clinic and in the work of the Defence AARTS Project in our Centre. I hope you'll excuse my using a poem of my own, which allows me room to discuss how writing it trained my own attentions, as well as to speculate on how its reading might widen the horizon of attention for a reader – including, perhaps, the kind of reading that might be undertaken by a physician or healthcare worker.

Here is the poem (which is untitled):

> he turns his hand and brushes the back
> of it against the back of mine. he lifts his
> hand then does that again. he reaches up
> and clasps the seam of my vest between
> his thumb and fingers. he pulls his hand
> away. he reaches up and does that again.
> he watches his hand and separates his
> fingers. he watches my hand and opens
> his fist, then closes his fist. he closes his
> fist around my finger. he opens his hand.
> he closes his hand around his hand then
> around one finger. he opens his hand.
> he brushes his hand against my chest.
> he lifts his hand and then softly he does
> that again.

As you might guess from reading this, I wrote it as a new mother. It emerged from the days I spent sitting with my son in his first months, the months of a fleeting maternity leave, in which it felt enough – and indeed absolutely necessary – to do nothing for long stretches of time but watch the smallest movements of my son's face, body and hands. I sometimes wondered in this period how to begin writing about an experience which was both mundane and utterly consuming. Flourishes of language of any kind did not seem true to the real nature of those stretched out hours, their circumscription, their intensified focus and their repletion. Indeed, the experience was so complete that there was no need to write at all – and yet there was also a desire to 'keep' an experience which, for all its 'sameness', was constantly changing form and (moment by moment, week by week) slipping away. My search for the language of this poem was a search for a way of knowing and addressing that constancy of emergence and loss.

Schleifer has written extensively on the relationship between the pragmatics of haptic development – 'the history of the hand,' he calls it in *Intangible Materialism* – and cognitive/narrative development, based upon the work of Charles Sanders Peirce (2009: 97-126), which has an important role in the pragmatics of understanding in the essay to follow. The work of the hand, Peirce argues, is closely imbricated with the linguistic function of attention; it is a site of the pragmatic power of language in general and the discursive arts more particularly. We can find this in attending to the ways this poem helps delineate the forms of attention arising from the engagement with the arts. How might a reader encounter this poem, what might they find in it? The language is simple and repetitive, the vocabulary minimal. Sentences are not differentiated by capital letters; lines are scarcely broken by the white space of the page. Perhaps for a reader unused to this kind of linguistic austerity there will be a felt sense correlating with what is difficult about new motherhood: frustration with its limited horizons, its 'smallness'. To tolerate this, the poem suggests, is to allow one's own attention to be fine-tuned by the unfolding significance of each gesture, both haptic and discursive, the way each gesture crosses a threshold of knowledge and expression – this is the same allowance that lets me and, at best, the poem's reader, be immersed in the experience of mothering. But for the presence of the single adjective – a single verbal gesture – in the final line, 'softly', the poem doesn't offer assertions of value, or qualitative standpoints. From the position of immersion, which is the work of the convergence of language and haptic gesture, these are unnecessary and often impossible. Indeed, for a long time I toyed with removing 'softly' for this very reason. But its appearance offers something else: narrative shape, the sense of release, the small moment of sweetness that comes at the moment of stepping back and feeling emotion returned as gestures open into intention.

Interestingly, the making of the poem had another layer, when I had the opportunity to work in a letterpress studio for a couple of days (letterpress printmaking is also, incidentally, one thread of the Defence ARRTS program we run). In this, my hands were working. I hand-set the poem's letters one by one in lead type, rolled paper and cloth through the press with minute adjustments each time, then slowly dissassembled the type to put it away. The painstaking and repetitive work was not unlike the work of parenting an infant, and I was returned to that sense of immersion in minute differentiations, which now began to characterise the physical appearance of the poem on the printed pages, evoking again the very differentiations I felt in my son's touch, my son's hands.

Later I gave a friend one of the resulting prints – a copy of the poem on calico. Months after I gave it to her we had lunch and she took the crumpled cloth out of her bag to show me. She said she'd meant to put it up on a wall but had liked having it with her, saying it felt 'like having a security blanket'. It seemed that her reading of the poem – her close attention to the poem's own forms of attention – had worked to take her as reader into the affect of the maternal bond, the social bond of touching, a security made of attentiveness in itself. If we understand the connection made in such an experience as purely emotional and spontaneous, we miss the work of systematic reasoning that is fundamental to both the writing and reading of the poem (and indeed, to the construction and reception of any artwork, narrative, or personal account). Schleifer's essay here, like his chapter on hands and poetry in *Intangible Materialism*, helps us to apprehend, understand and heighten our facility with that work.

Work in Medical Humanities by Ronald Schleifer

Publications

Books and Monographs

Pain and Suffering. New York and London: Routledge, 2014. (Translated into Chinese: Central China Normal University Press, 2017.)

The Chief Concern of Medicine: The Integration of the Medical Humanities and Narrative Knowledge into Medical Practices. Co-authored with Jerry Vannatta, MD. Ann Arbor: University of Michigan Press, 2013.

'The Role of Narrative in the Everyday Practice of Medicine: A Symposium in Seven Parts.' Co-authored with Jerry Vannatta and Sheila Crow. A monograph published by the *Journal of the Oklahoma State Medical Association* 2010.

Intangible Materialism: The Body, Scientific Knowledge, and the Power of Language by Ronald Schleifer. Minneapolis: University of Minnesota Press, 2009.

Medicine and Humanistic Understanding: The Significance of Narrative in Medical Practices, Co-authored with Jerry Vannatta, MD, and Sheila Crow. Philadelphia: University of Pennsylvania Press, 2005, a DVD-ROM publication.

Culture and Cognition: The Boundaries of Literary and Scientific Inquiry. Co-authored with Robert Con Davis and Nancy Mergler. Ithaca: Cornell University Press, 1992.

Special Section: *Theories of Corporeal Experience in Experimental Literary Practices* (compiled with Tatiana Venediktova), *New Literary Observer*, Moscow, Fall 2015.

Chapters and Articles

'Medical Professionalism: Using Literary Narrative to Explore and Evaluate Medical Professionalism' (co-authors Dr Casey Hester and Dr Jerry Vannatta), in *The Palgrave Handbook for Literature and Medicine*, ed. Stephanie Hilger, forthcoming 2017.

'The Semiotics of Sensation: A. J. Greimas and the Experience of Meaning,' *Semiotica* 214 (2017): 173-93.

'Enhancing Physician Empathy: Optimizing Learner Potential for Narrative Transportation' (co-author with Dr Casey Hester) in a special issue of *Enthymema* 16, on 'Medicine and Narrative' ed. by Elena Fratto, (2016): 105-18.

'The Terrible Facticity of Pain: Semiotics and Sensate Experience' (translated into Russian by Andrey Logutov), *New Literary Observer*, Moscow, 308 (2015): 16-27.

'The Poetics of Tourette's Syndrome: Language, Neurobiology, and Poetry,' in *Literature, Speech Disorders, and Disability: Talking Normal*, edited by Chris Eagle (New York: Routledge, 2014), pp. 137-61. This chapter originally appeared in *New Literary History* 32 (2001): 563-84.

'Narrative Knowledge, *Phronesis*, and Paradigm-Based Medicine,' *Narrative* 20 (2012): 64-86.

'The Chief Concern of Medicine: Narrative, *Phronesis*, and the History of Present Illness' (co-author with Dr Jerry Vannatta), in *Binocular Vision: Narrative and Metaphor in Medicine*, ed. Michael Hanne, a special issue of *Genre* 44 (2011): 335-47.

'Modalities of Science: *Phronesis*, Narrative, and the Practices of Medicine,' *Danish Yearbook of Philosophy*, 44 (2009): 77-101.

'The Logic of Diagnosis: Peirce, Literary Narrative, and the History of Present Illness' (co-author with Dr Jerry Vannatta), *The Journal of Medicine and Philosophy*, 31 (2006): 363-85.

'Helping Medical Students Understand Post-partum Psychosis through the Prism of 'The Yellow Wallpaper' by Charlotte Perkins Gilman,' (co-authored: Phebe Tucker, Sheila Crow, Anne Cuccio, Jerry B. Vannatta. *Academic Psychiatry*, 28 (Fall 2004): 247-50.

'Literature and Medicine: A Curriculum for Stimulating the Moral Imagination,' (co-author with Dr Jerry Vannatta), *Journal of the Oklahoma State Medical Association*, 93 (2000): 56-59.

'The Music of Pain: Semiotics, Facticity, and the Possibility of Representing Pain,' paper presented at the Centre for Creative and Cultural Research, University of Canberra, May 2017.

Workshops

Among other venues, Professor Schleifer has participated in workshops on Literature and Medicine sponsored by the Oklahoma Humanities Council, ongoing Medical Education at the University of Oklahoma, and other workshops and lectures at the University of Illinois, Nanjing University, University of Bristol, Shanghai International Studies University, the University of Illinois, Moscow State University, Harbin Institute of Technology (China), Shanxi Medical University, University of Missouri, University of Copenhagen, Colorado College, University of Lausanne, University of Tulsa, University of Aberdeen, and Georgia Tech University.

Practical Reasoning: How the Experience of the Humanities can Help Train Doctors

Ronald Schleifer

This essay is part of my contribution to the growing area in higher education in the United States that focuses on the medical humanities as part of the training of medical students and the ongoing training of practicing physicians, but it also indicates the interdisciplinary value of the humanities more broadly. The medical humanities can be defined as interdisciplinary studies and teaching that draw upon the creative and intellectual work of disciplines outside of biomedicine to contribute to the education of physicians and healthcare workers. These disciplines include areas in the humanities I outline later in this essay: literary studies, history, art studies, philosophy and social sciences such as anthropology, cultural studies, sociology. In this essay, I argue vigorously that the humanities can be understood as being as systematically rigorous as the nomological (or 'law-like') sciences that have been the mainstay of training in medical schools since the beginnings of formal medical education in the early twentieth century. This has recently come to be called 'evidence-based medicine.'

Two practicing and teaching physicians – both of whom work in internal medicine – contribute significantly to this argument. The first is Jerry

Vannatta, MD, with whom I have worked closely. For almost twenty years we team-taught a course on 'Literature and Medicine,' primarily for pre-med students but also for second-year medical students and in workshops for practicing physicians. We have co-authored a number of books and essays, perhaps most significantly *The Chief Concern of Medicine: The Integration of the Medical Humanities and Narrative Knowledge into Medical Practices*, which appeared in 2013. The second is Rita Charon, MD, Ph.D. (in literary studies), who teaches and practices internal medicine at the Columbia University College of Physicians and Surgeons. At Columbia she is the Founder and Executive Director of the Program in Narrative Medicine. Her most famous book is *Narrative Medicine: Honoring the Stories of Illness*. In some ways, she is unique in the field with training in both medicine and literary studies. Still, what she has done in her combination of disciplinary trainings Dr. Vannatta and I have done in our collaborative work, bringing together literary studies and medical pedagogy.

It is the argument in this essay – as it is the argument of *The Chief Concern of Medicine* – that like the disciplines of the nomological sciences of biomedicine, which systematically pursue the strict *quantification and formulation* of the natural phenomena they study, and like the social sciences of anthropology, sociology, and psychology, which systematically pursue retrospective *explanations* of the social phenomena they study, the humanities systematically develop what the late nineteenth-century American philosopher and polymath Charles Sanders Peirce calls 'habits of thought,' engendered through systematic disciplinary study of language, history, philosophy, and art forms, to develop certain *forms of attention* that allow people, habitually, to notice certain kinds of things that they would otherwise miss. Here is what I mean by 'discipline' in this essay: not simply acquiring a body of knowledge, but developing habitual attention and skills of understanding and action that allow us to contribute to the communities in which we live and work. More particularly, in this essay I focus on the systematic understanding of narrative, the 'narrative knowledge' in the subtitle of *The Chief Concern of Medicine*. Narrative knowledge is a special kind of information in which the whole is greater than the sum of the parts. Because of this, to systematically obtain it, a person must be trained in the particular *form* of this knowledge: namely, the 'schemas' by which we grasp what one linguist calls the 'meaningful whole' of any message.

In an interview, Dr. Charon describes the function of attending to and understanding narrative in her practice as a physician. This description, I think, offers a precise framework for understanding how the humanities can help train physicians and, indeed, other healthcare workers. 'This interest we [medical educators pursuing 'narrative medicine'] have in narrative knowledge and narrative methods,' she noted, is not an abstract, scholarly interest alone. It's a very practical interest. There is a very concrete, direct relationship between narrative knowledge and clinical action. Indeed, we are interested in helping our students and doctors understand things for their own purposes. We're even interested in helping them reflect on their experience and feel better for it. I'm happy when my students or the doctors who study with us feel better by virtue of their narrative training, but that's not enough. My goal in giving them narrative training is to enable them to act more effectively with their patients. So, the increase in the narrative skills of recognizing there's a story to be heard, eliciting it, being curious about what's unsaid, putting it together in some way, trying provisional hypotheses to see 'Did I get this right?', and being moved oneself by what's heard, all of these things culminate in the doctor then being able to act on the patient's behalf with more vigor, with more purpose, with more investment than they otherwise would.

I talk sometimes about how we have to honor the narratives we hear, and this is a very active thing. People tell us very private, frightening things about themselves, and we, because we have skill and also because we have power, are privileged to hear these things. Sometimes they are things we don't want to know about, like child abuse, nonetheless,

> we hear about these things. We have duties toward these things we hear, and for doctors, I think there are twin duties. One duty is to honor what's been said, which is to say, not to trivialize it, not to dismiss it, not to forget it; and then we have the duty to act. By virtue of knowing what I now know, what must I do? I think this is where narrative training increases the professionalism of doctors, yes? (Vannatta, Schleifer, Crow 2005: Chapter 4, screen 8 [video])

In this discussion of the work of narrative knowledge in medical practice, Dr. Charon presents six qualities of attention and understanding. Narrative knowledge, she notes, requires that a doctor

- recognizes there is a story to be heard;
- elicits the story;
- is curious about what is 'unsaid';
- attempts to grasp it as a 'meaningful whole';
- develops provisional hypotheses of its meaning: 'Did I get this right?';
- is moved by what is heard; all of which culminate in the doctor then being able to act on the patient's behalf.

These qualities, I am suggesting, help accomplish in the practice of medicine what Aristotle called *phronesis*, which is usually translated as 'practical reasoning' or 'practical wisdom.' In *The Nicomachean Ethics* his chief example of *phronesis* is the accomplished physician. (Aristotle's father was a physician.) Here, then, is the global argument of this essay:

The Argument. Almost everyone, from ancient times to the present, agrees that one of the most important skills in doctoring is the practical reasoning of *phronesis*; and almost everyone agrees it is a skill obtained only through long experience. In this essay I argue that the humanities teach us to apprehend and learn from experience more quickly and with precision, efficacy, and care.

Humanities and Experience

I begin my exposition with a short anecdote. Several years ago, I was teaching literature and medicine at a small liberal arts college in the United States. Near the end of the second week, a young woman literature major came to my office seething with anger. 'Look what you're trying to do,' she almost shouted at me. 'You're trying to make literature *practical*!' I start with this anecdote because in this essay I examine the concept and phenomenology of *experience* – and especially *practical* experience – that, I claim, is a defining feature of the humanities, particularly in relation to what we, in the humanities, have to teach medical students and physicians.

By way of beginning in earnest, let me get practical without, I hope, provoking the kind of anger my student expressed. Recently, in 2015, the national examination for medical school in the United States – the Medical College Admission

Test, or 'MCAT' – changed format. Darrell Kirch, MD, the President of the American Association of Medical Colleges, the organization that administers the MCAT, announced in an open letter to pre-med students the rationale for the change. He noted that

> Our profession increasingly recognizes that our current health care model needs to do more to promote prevention and wellness for patients. Our nation is growing, aging, and becoming increasingly diverse, so physicians of the future must be more culturally competent. And patients, especially those with chronic conditions, will need a 'medical home' in which their providers work as unified teams to coordinate their care, instead of the current fragmented approach.
>
> * * *
>
> Thinking about the rapid increases in medical knowledge brings me to another feature of the 2015 exam: the new 'Critical Analysis and Reasoning Skills' section, which is designed to help medical schools assess how you think by asking you to analyze passages from a wide range of disciplines, including ethics, philosophy, cultural studies, and even population health. No longer is it humanly possible to memorize every fact relevant to the practice of medicine. What is more important for physicians of the future is an ability to think critically and to have the necessary reasoning

> skills to know where to seek answers and how to solve problems in the clinical environment. (2012: https://www.aamc.org/newsroom/reporter/march2012/276772/word.html)

These issues of focusing on care, developing co-ordinated medical teams, and training physicians in critical thinking are all in the province of the humanities (as well as psychology and sociology, which is the focus of a second new section of the MCAT). For these issues the concept of experience is crucial, and my title gives two meanings of the word 'experience': namely how we experience the humanities and how the human sciences analyze and teach us – and, most importantly, can teach physicians – to understand experience in a richer and more reflective way.

In my recent work I have been borrowing the term *schema* from cognitive psychology. Schemas are systematic patterns of cognition, patterns of how we put together experience. The grammar of language is one such schema, as is the pattern of furniture in a classroom that allows us to immediately recognize it as a classroom even when we never saw this particular room before. Another schema – important for this essay – is the pattern of events in a narrative that allows even children as young as four years old to recognize that a story is not well formed (Polkinghorne 1988: 20). Recently psychologists and others have been arguing that schemas organize, if often in a provisional fashion, present experience itself by means of actively conditioning *attention and expectation*. Such conditioning, as Todd Gurekis and Robert Goldstone note, is the work of schemas, which 'allow us to predict or infer unknown information in completely new situations' (2011: 725). An example: native speakers of English attend to and expect that the changing tone or pitch of spoken language only signifies on the level of sentences: a rising tone signifies a question. On the level of particular words, tone is disregarded: it does not call attention to itself as such and does not fit into the expected schematic organization of sounds of English. (The rising sound of one word – e.g., *What?* – indicates that it is a one-word sentence.) In many Asian languages, such as Chinese, the tone of particular words is a distinctive feature, a mode of differentiating one meaning from another. It does so because the schema of any language teaches us to automatically pay attention to certain sounds and to expect to hear those sounds. While we learn languages from our environment – hence its differences between Chinese and English – the propensity to acquire language is an inherited human quality, like the natural tendency to walk, or, as I mention later in this essay, the natural tendency to organize experience in relation to narrative schemas.

Moreover, it is precisely schemas of experience that allow the humanities to conceive of itself as a discipline and, in turn, be integrated within medical training and practice. In 2014, I published a short book entitled *Pain and Suffering*. My book argues that the phenomenon – which is to say the *experience* – of human pain is best understood in relation to *schemas of experience.* That is, schemas explain the remarkable fact that very similar somatic injuries – even in the same person – give rise to remarkably different experiences of pain under different circumstances. Thus, in a powerful account of pain, Melanie Thernstrom describes the complexity of pain experience altogether. 'Is pain sensation, emotion, or idea?,' she asks.

> Is it a product of biology or culture? If it is primarily a biological phenomenon, then why does it seem to vary so much from person to person and from culture to culture? If it is primarily a cultural one, then why does it seem so universal? After all, there is a word for headache in every language, ancient and modern. When the ancient Babylonian describes the headache that envelops like a garment, we know exactly what he means. (2010: 281)

It is the complexity of experience – including psychological and neurological schemas that condition experience altogether – that is the focus of the humanities. When we study the 'style' of Cezanne, the discursive strategies of Toni Morrison, the economic or social or personal patterns of historical behavior, the characteristic major-seventh chords in Cole Porter, even the standardized procedures of logic, we study the form and power of schemas of experience, forms and power of attention and expectation. Moreover, it is our focus on experience that allows the disciplines of the humanities to help train physicians. This is most clear when we remember that in my own discipline of literary studies that the term *experience* is related to the word *aesthetic* as derived from the Greek *αἰσθητικός* (*aisthetikos*), meaning 'esthetic, sensitive, sentient', which in turn was derived from αἰσθάνομαι (*aisthanomai*), meaning 'I perceive, feel, sense': thus aesthetics – and the rarefied notion of 'aesthetic experience' – can be understood, simply, within the general category of experience itself (see Schleifer 2018).

Narrative and Medicine

To discuss the humanities as a discipline focusing on experience, I'd like to begin with my work in literature and medicine. As I already mentioned, for almost two decades Dr. Jerry Vannatta and I taught a course that brings together the humanities and medicine. This course came about because of an experience Jerry had in his practice, which was related to Toni Morrison's great novel, *Beloved*. The novel, one of the most important in American literature, traces a family of African American slaves in their lives right before the American Civil War. It narrates the life and experience of a slave woman, Sethe, who finds life as a slave so hateful that she kills her infant daughter to prevent her from living a life of slavery. What is so powerful about the novel is the way it makes us empathize with this woman who commits such a terrible crime. It is an important book because it allows its readers to feel and *experience* the life of slavery. Before reading this book, I – like many fellow Americans – only had the most abstract sense of the terrible condition of chattel slavery in our country. Morrison's book makes this terrible time in our history – my history too, even though my grandparents came to United States from Europe fifty years after the end of slavery – terribly *real* for those who read it. The experience of this novel changed Dr. Vannatta's practice. 'I came to this whole interest in narrative, literature, and the practice of medicine,' he noted in an interview,

> through an experience I had in my own practice. I'm a general internist, and I had an elderly African American woman who came back to the office for an office visit after having been in the hospital. I didn't get to know her real well in the hospital because she was cared for primarily by the residents and the medical students on my service, but when she came back for an office visit, I was providing the care. And she rapidly told me that she was having trouble getting her medications. As I was interacting with her, there was just really no connection being made. That makes me so uncomfortable when I'm really not connecting with the patient, so, as I usually do when I'm not connecting well, I backed up and sort of took a psychosocial history. I basically just said, 'Tell me about your life.'

She began to tell me a story about having grown up in east Texas on a sharecropping farm where her father was a sharecropper, and he, when she was fifteen, made her marry a man who was twenty-one. It really wasn't the man she wanted to marry; she was in love with a sixteen year-old, but he made her marry the twenty-one year-old because he could provide for a living. In fact, she said to me during the story that 'he wasn't very good at making a living, but he was sure good at making babies,' and she had seventeen of them. And I thought at the time she said that, 'My goodness, that could have rolled right out of a wonderful novel or short story.' She went on to say that she, oftentimes to make ends meet, walked two miles to a white man's house and two miles back to do domestic work. And she told me that sometimes the white man would give her a dozen eggs, and sometimes he would give her a two-gallon pail of milk to carry back to the family. And then she looked at me and said, 'Doctor, have you ever carried a two-gallon pail of milk two miles?' And, in fact, I did grow up on a farm, and I can remember carrying those galvanized pails of water around the farm to the chickens and whatnot, and I could just see that wire handle just burying itself and cutting into her hand.

But more importantly, I was thinking that I was seeing her carrying this pail of milk on a dusty, sort of rocky road, probably with not very good shoes. And as I was thinking about her feet, making this journey back, I began to think of this novel, Toni Morrison's novel, *Beloved*, which I had just read a few months earlier, at that time, the most remarkable novel I had ever read, a very disturbing story about slavery in America. And the protagonist, Sethe, is running from slavery. She's pregnant, she's trying to escape, and she's tired and she's about to deliver a baby, and she's hiding up under a bush and a little white girl finds her. One of the things that's striking about that scene is her swollen, bleeding and pussy, infected feet. And that image of those feet came back to me just in a flood, and the emotions that I had felt, I think, when I read the novel were seemingly stored in memory. And along with the image of the feet, these emotions came flooding back to me. And the remarkable thing that happened in the room was that those emotions were available to me to be able to connect with this lady, not that she was a slave, but in some way she was telling me a story about her economic enslavement and somehow they connected. I don't know how that works, but nonetheless, it happened. It was an experience that was dramatic for me, and from that point on, we began to make a more meaningful connection, and we rapidly sort of problem solved her ability to buy her medications and get them so that she could

> take them. And at the end of the interaction, we stood up to leave and a remarkable thing happened, which usually doesn't happen in my practice, which is we embraced. And she knew that a wonderful relationship had begun, and so did I. (quoted in Vannatta, Schleifer, Crow 2005: Chapter 2, Screen 27 [video])

In this interview – indeed, in his experience with his patient – Jerry notes that he experienced a 'flood' of emotion that allowed him 'to connect' to his patient, although, as he says, 'I don't know how that works.' Later, in a book that we wrote together, *The Chief Concern of Medicine*, Jerry and I try to understand how this works, which is to say how an 'art' narrative – such as Morrison's *Beloved* – and even an everyday narrative, such as that of his patient, give rise to experience, knowledge, and social connection. Even the patient's observation, in the midst of an anxious and fretful meeting with her physician, that her husband 'wasn't very good at making a living, but he was sure good at making babies,' draws our attention to the formal patterns of language – here, the play on the word 'making' used figuratively in terms of 'making a living' and literally in terms of 'making babies' – suggesting that the experience narrative provokes can be analyzed in terms of linguistic strategies (here a strategy conditioned by what I take to be a universal aspect of languages schemas, the opposition between literal and figurative meanings).

But most importantly, the whole experience of 'connecting' to a patient – which means engagement with attentive listening, attentive questioning, and the ethics of engaged care – grows out of the manner in which the humanities in general aim at systematically accounting for experience, which includes the experience of knowledge and the experience of meaning. In his *Autobiography*, William Carlos Williams devotes a chapter, entitled 'The Practice,' to describing parallels between his career as a physician and his career as a poet, in which he nicely delineates what Jerry means by 'connecting.' Attending to the language of his patients and to that of his poems, he notes that 'the difficulty is to catch the evasive life of the thing, to phrase the words in such a way that stereotype will yield a moment of insight' (1951: 359). In Jerry's encounter with his patient – and, perhaps, most notably, in his encounter with his patient's words – he discovers a moment of insight by grasping his patient's experience in a manner analogous to the way in which Morrison delineates the experience of her heroine in her discursive art. (In class we analyze the strategies – and discursive schemas – by which Morrison achieves this end.) In this way, Morrison's art informs Jerry's engagement with someone who seems, in narrating her story, more than someone simply inhabiting the 'role' of patient: stereotype is transformed to insight. In this timely project of momentary (but lasting) insight, the humanities are unlike the timeless formulas of the nomological (or 'law like') sciences and evidence-based medicine and unlike the retrospective explanations of evolutionary biology and medical epidemiology. (For a catalogue of the functioning of these disciplinary modalities see Schleifer 2009).

Not long after this experience, Jerry got in touch with me, and for nineteen years we taught 'Literature and Medicine' to undergraduate pre-med students, second-year medical students, and in workshops for physicians and other healthcare workers. In these courses we worked to help develop practical interviewing and diagnostic skills, skills in what Aristotle calls *phronesis* or 'practical reasoning.' We did so by pursuing what we call 'schema-based medicine,' which is parallel to 'evidence-based medicine' that has been widely practiced in the United States and Western Europe for the past twenty years. Evidence-based medicine has come to assume two forms. The strictest of these forms is what Dr. Atul Gawande describes as 'the idea that nothing ought to be introduced into practice unless it has been properly tested and proved effective by research centers, preferably through a double blind, randomized controlled trial' (2007: 188). A second sense of evidence-based medicine pursues a less restrictive approach where 'evidence' consists of matters of fact that are gathered through more general observation of what happens in less rigidly controlled situations (i.e., less strictly controlled than laboratory testing). In both cases, however, evidence-based medicine eschews experience in favor of more-or-less precise protocols of scientific 'discipline.' These sciences assume that the facts and events they study – the *evidence* of evidence-based science – are 'commensurable,' which means that *any* falling object will behave like any other, or any neuron like any other. Thus, Valerie Gray Hardcastle notes in her book, *The Myth of Pain*, that 'the neurons that make up the brain are essentially identical across all animals in the kingdom' (1999: 63), and she virtually begins her book with the assertion that all pain is the 'same': 'all pains are physical and localizable and . . . all are created equal' (1999: 7). On the other hand, the schemas of cognitive psychology explicitly pursue the systematic study of experience without the assumption that 'commensurability' is the starting point of knowledge; and the particular disciplines of the humanities implicitly pursue such systematic study under the categories of history, aesthetics, and the *experience* of understanding altogether in philosophy, semiotics, and, I would say, the cultural studies Dr. Kirch mentions in his letter to pre-med students.

This is important because from ancient times until the present it has been often argued and almost always assumed that the most important clinical skills of an accomplished physician can only be gained through long experience. Aristotle described these skills under the term *phronesis* or 'practical reason' (though sometimes it is also translated as 'practical wisdom') and most commentators on *phronesis* – a powerful and eloquent example is

Martha Nussbaum (1990) – have agreed that there is no systematic way in which *phronesis* can be taught the way the facts and methods of the nomological and empirical sciences can be taught: it can only be obtained, it is assumed, through long first-hand experience.

As I mentioned already, in 2013 Jerry and I published *The Chief Concern of Medicine*. The purpose of the book, as the subtitle states, is *The Integration of the Medical Humanities and Narrative Knowledge into Medical Practices*. In our work we argue that experience itself – and medical *phronesis* itself – can be taught as carefully as the protocols of science can be taught by making explicit the schemas that condition and shape experience. Such engagements with the schemas of experience in relation to narrative texts, we have found, help students develop strategies for certain habits of action. One of the things schemas create are habits of action: thus we ride a bike almost without thinking just as we recognize a room as a classroom seemingly without thinking. In our book we set forth a small number of schemas in order to develop a notion of 'schema-based medicine' parallel to 'evidence-based medicine.' They include schemas of narrative based upon the work of the semiotician A. J. Greimas; schemas of diagnosis based upon the logic of abduction (or 'hypothesis formation') of Charles Sanders Peirce; and schemas of behavior based upon Aristotle's virtue ethics. Moreover, we set forth a set of practical schemas in the form of checklists based upon Dr. Gawande's book *The Checklist Manifesto*, that is a framework designed to help students and physicians to develop habits of action in their interactions with patients. It is striking that a practicing surgeon, Dr. Atul Gawande, has written a book about the practical usefulness of checklists for airlines, large-scale construction projects, and his most important audience, physicians and healthcare workers. I return to his book at the end of this essay.

Behind our program in *The Chief Concern of Medicine* is the assumption, which I want to explicitly articulate in this essay, that experience is not, in fact, necessarily *immediate*, but rather mediated through schemas of perception, experience, and apprehension: semiotic schemas of attention and understanding, which are precisely the means by which the humanities can help train physicians (see Schleifer 2017). That is, it is the work of the humanities in general to study and unpack these schemas; more particularly, to study what the literary critic Paul de Man has described as the 'non-perceptual, linguistic moment' in the verbal arts that calls for *reading* (1994: 107) – by which he means active interpretation – rather than immediate, intuitive apprehension. De Man does not say so, but I have learned in the practical work of the medical humanities – and particularly in the work of convincing physicians and others trained in the systematic sciences – that the processes of 'reading' de Man describes are organized around the schemas of experience I am setting forth here. Training in recognizing and utilizing such schemas is precisely the means by which the humanities can help train physicians.

Narrative Schemas

The first of the schemas Jerry and I discuss in *The Chief Concern of Medicine* is the 'narrative knowledge' of our subtitle, which is, in fact, a way of apprehending and shaping experience conditioned by *schemas of perception and apprehension* governing attention and expectation. In fact, there is good and convincing evidence that schemas of narration are part of our human inheritance shaped by evolutionary adaptations (see Boyd 2009). In any case, clinical medicine – including primitive methods of people caring for one another in communities – is basically organized around the story, what contemporary medicine in the United States calls the narrative History of Present Illness (HPI) that the patient (or sometimes others) almost always brings to the doctor. This is usually a story with a beginning and a middle, but patients come to physicians in hopes of discovering or developing the 'end' of their particular story – they come with what Alasdair MacIntyre calls 'a not-yet-completed narrative' (1984: 223) – and it is precisely in the negotiation and apprehension of the 'end' or 'chief concern' of the patient's story that narrative knowledge can serve medical practices. The more competent the physician is in self-consciously understanding narrative discourse – in apprehending the patient's story – the more accurately he or she will diagnose patients, in relation to the *chief complaint* – the first thing American physicians record on the patient's chart – but even more importantly in relation to what we are calling their *chief concern.* (Hence the title of our book.) If a patient's chief complaint is, for instance, long-term pain in his shoulder, his chief concern might be that he may lose his job or his fear of arthritis; it might be his concern for his relationship with his domestic partner; it might be a fear of life-threatening diseases. We argue that the chief concern should, like the chief complaint, be a category added to the patient's chart (the History and Physical Exam): in this way physicians would be required to make it part of the medical interview. Discernment of the chief concern is accomplished through careful engagements with narrative structures and narrative ethics that are most powerfully achieved in the careful reading of literary texts and the careful study of humanistic schemas. In our book we distinguish between the 'art' narratives of literature – which, we argue, aim at organizing aesthetic effects and provoking vicarious experience rather than practical communication in a particular situation – and ordinary narratives encountered in everyday life, which aim at discovering and encouraging practical action in the world.

Here I do not have the space to describe schemas of narrative and of ethics in any detail, but I thought I might offer an example of an ordinary narrative as opposed to an 'art' narrative, such as *Beloved.* This is a narrative from Jerry's clinical practice. It describes a depressed patient who was hospitalized for abdominal pain. The interns and residents on Jerry's service could find no somatic causes of her pain, and dismissed her as 'a crock.' When Jerry came to interview her, she hardly answered at all, and in the face of her unresponsiveness, Jerry asked her about her family. Here is Jerry's account of this clinical encounter.

> 'Tell me about your family. Where did you grow up?' I heard a story about her mother, her sister and two brothers in North Carolina. She shared the story of her leaving town after high school graduation in search of adventure. After losing several jobs, she found herself in a homeless shelter in Indianapolis, where she met her future husband. She described how he convinced her to jump a freight train with him and go find work, and soon they found themselves in Oklahoma City, still out of work, hungry, and caring for a three-month-old baby.
>
> At the pause in her story, I said, 'You told me of your family, but you didn't mention your father.' She looked down, frowned and stated in a barely audible voice, 'He wasn't very nice to me.' After a long silence, she continued. 'He hurt me and was dirty with me.'

'Did he hurt you physically?'

'Yes, with a belt, many times.'

'Did he sexually hurt you too?'

Looking down and in a very quiet voice, she replied, 'Yeah.'

'I am sorry that happened to you; I can imagine that it is very difficult to live with.'

'Yes, but I think things are better now.'

(adapted from Schleifer & Vannatta 2013: 342-43)

From this point Jerry learned that this young woman was frightened by her husband, who hadn't physically abused her but often made threatening gestures with his belt. And because of this knowledge – because he was able to discern the fuller narrative she was communicating – he was able to help her find appropriate care, attending to both her physical and psycho-social circumstances.

In this narrative, the patient presents her doctor with a not-yet-completed story, and in striving to complete it – in striving to transform the stereotype, by which the interns and residents understood this patient, into insight – the physician in this narrative focuses upon his patient's chief concern: what her condition (or situation) *means* to her. Here, that concern is unspoken – perhaps precisely in the way that trauma, such as this young woman experienced, maintains itself in silence and confusion. In this clinical situation it is the work of the physician to facilitate its articulation, if possible, and to *hear* its articulation, so that as a treatment path is developed from this point, it is developed with respect to the patient's narrative, as fully achieved as possible. In this, the facilitation of the patient's narrative is, in fact, an important strategy in clinical medicine insofar as it allows patient and physician together to grasp the patient's concern in the context – both immediate and long-term – in which she finds herself. In order to provide treatment that is responsive in this way, several things are necessary. First of all, it is necessary that the physician understand that a patient's concern is as important to his work as is her chief complaint. When medicine conceives itself as a physiological science, it imagines that the 'complaint' is the object of its work: this is the focus of the interns and residents in Jerry's service. To make the patient's *chief concern* as important as his *chief complaint* – to *formally* require its explicit articulation in the chart in the same way that the chief complaint is a heading that has to be filled in – would transform the physician's goal in taking the patient's history.

More than this general concern is a second thing necessary for the understanding of the patient's story, namely a sense of what is *unsaid* in the narrative. As we have seen, Dr. Charon describes one of the things a physician must do is to be 'curious about what is unsaid.' The only way to be attentive to what is missing from a narrative is to understand the structure and elements of narrative in general, the *schemas* of narrative. That is, the possibility of noticing what is 'unsaid' in a patient's story requires an explicit understanding of the necessary elements of narrative wholeness. Even young children recognize ill-formed narratives without understanding why, but in order to achieve a full understanding of a story's 'concern,' one needs to have a sense of what might be missing. That is, if narratives have a structure just as sentences have a structure – scholars in the humanities talk about 'narrative grammars' – this would explain why we recognize ill-formed narratives. In a similar fashion, if narratives have a generalized purpose – a function that narrative serves in human affairs – then we can equally notice when something is missing from a narrative. One of the functions of narrative, scholars in evolutionary adaptation have argued, is to help figure out what to do in the future. In fact, Francis Steen argues that adaptive narrative structures are recognizable in the 'playfights' of rhesus monkeys (2005: 97-100), which serve to teach the younger monkeys to 'construe' possible ends of their actions. In their play, he argues, the monkeys exhibit 'the development of proto-narratives in the form of multiple . . . strategies with an underlying structural design' so that 'rhesus playfighting . . . has the *structure* of fictive narratives' (2005: 98).

One simple schema of narrative we set forth is a small set – a 'checklist' as we describe it – of necessary but not sufficient narrative agents in any story that is felt to be 'whole.' While there is much controversy concerning narrative structures and forms in the humanities, we believe simple practical checklists of elements of the schemas we study in the humanities can aid in physicians' everyday encounters with patients just as simple practical checklists set forth by evidence-based guides (such as found in the British publication, *Clinical Evidence Concise*) aid in the everyday practices of medicine. One such checklist we set forth describes four roles in narrative: the hero, the object of desire, the helper, the opponent. We can see these roles in the characters of Elizabeth Bennett (the hero), Mr. Darcy (the object of desire), her uncle and aunt Gardner (the helper), and Wickham (the opponent) in the agent-actors of *Pride and Prejudice*. But in the narrative of Jerry's unresponsive patient, the 'opponent' role – embodied by the patient's father – is 'anticipated' by Jerry in his question and discovered to have been omitted. Such anticipation is governed by the active attention and expectation of schemas.

In Steen's description of rhesus playfighting (although he does not use our narrative schema), he notes that 'rhesus macaques occupy a first-person role in an exciting and aboriginal drama. By fighting with a larger and more experienced individual, younger monkeys are challenged to anticipate their opponent's moves. To master this task, they must construe these moves in narrative terms and grasp the underlying plot' (2005: 98). By 'moves,' Steen is taking up the vocabulary of Donald Symons in a filmed analysis of rhesus macaque play-fighting (1977): Steen describes such 'moves' as 'behavioral sequences' that can be isolated in terms of '*length* and *complexity*' (2005: 97); the macaques 'generate complex behaviors that consist in moves drawn from a large repertoire, assembled into orderly and contextually contingent sequences designed to reach intermediate goals' (2005: 98). In this way, Steen describes a structural, schematic understanding of macaque play-fighting that, in his argument, can be understood as a *narrative* structure insofar as it allows the macaques to 'construe' – that is to say, generate 'behavioral predictions' of (2005: 98) – what is and what will be taking place. In a similar fashion, an understanding of the resources of narrative structures allowed Jerry to hear the 'unsaid' in his patient's story, and in doing so to work with her to figure out the best treatment for her condition. This understanding that narrative has a structure – among other things, a systematic and schematic array of actors – and that it has a generalized purpose – namely that it allows one to contemplate, judge, and play with possible future actions – is closely related to Charles Sanders Peirce's claim that one of the functions of language is to grasp, even in a provisional way, the 'law that will govern the future' (1931-1935, 1958: 1.23).

In this context, narrative can be understood in terms of necessary but not sufficient schemas, particularly insofar as narrative represents and – I argue – provokes experience itself. This last is the phenomenon of vicarious experience such as provoked by *Beloved* for Jerry. In fact, in the last twenty years, detailed and reproducible scientific experiments in cognitive science have demonstrated this effect of literary narrative. That is, quantitative and repeatable experiments have been conducted that demonstrate measurable increases of cognitive skills brought about by engagements with literary texts (e.g., qualities of experience, strategies of interaction, simply *knowledge* about other people), which would enhance the patient-physician relation. Reading of literary narrative, it has been found,

- promotes **empathetic responses** to the experience of others,
- enlarges the ability to recognize the separate values and understanding of others (experimenters call this **Theory of Mind**) and to act on that recognition in interaction with others, and
- develops **vicarious experience** (experimenters call this 'narrative transportation') that promotes knowledge of the lives of people of different backgrounds, social class, gender orientation, etc. (See Hester and Schleifer 2016 for a survey of these experiments and their usefulness in the training and practice of medicine.)

It is my contention that these measurable effects are a function of the engagement and enlargement of semiotic schemas.

Such schemas set forth a 'law' – the 'law that will govern the future' – that is provisional rather than *absolute* insofar as schemas, as one scholar notes, 'are ever changing and constantly updating, reflecting the ongoing stream of perception and thought in our mental lives' (Hardcastle 1999: 119). Moreover, the notion of the 'enlargement' of semiotic schemas should make this clear. Thus, Charles Taylor writes that

> language may be viewed as a structure of rules, or of possible formations and transformations. But . . . [particular speech acts] are not in a simple relation of subsumption with the rule to which they are submitted. They may be in conformity with it, or they may deviate. . . . Languages live only through successive renewals, each of which is a risk, for it runs the risk of not coming through this renewal unharmed. (1991: 176)

In this way, he is arguing that the schemas of the humanities – perhaps unlike the schemas of cognitive psychology – entertain possibilities of negotiation, just as a physician and patient can negotiate together the best 'outcomes' of a particular situation (what 'good health' might mean in any particular situation). The renewal and risk Taylor describes in relation to language rules – I would add they also exist in relation to rules/schemas of narrative – create opportunities of renewal and enlargement as well as risk. In any case, Jerry's educated guess about his patient was provisional in a sense related to Taylor's analysis: his patient's father could have been absent from her story for several different reasons – because of divorce, death, or overwork. But more generally, my larger argument about the nature of the humanities as a discipline is that it studies and makes explicit schemas of everyday experience, and it is knowledge about such schemas that can help physicians (and, indeed, all of us) attain the worldly wisdom of *phronesis* by means of practical semiotics and humanistic study more generally by allowing us to entertain and judge different scenarios of understanding and action.

I am arguing then that we conceive of the humanities as a discipline or disciplines of the schematic apprehensions of *experience* itself: the experience of art, of narrative, of *meaning* itself. In the discussion of *phronesis* in our book we cite Steen's argument that 'conscious perceptual experience is the fine-tuned product of hundreds of millions of years of mammalian evolution' (2005: 95). In this, he is suggesting that the *felt immediacy* of perception and experience can be understood as *mediated* by means of evolutionary adaptive schemas designed to order recurring patterns of experiential phenomena and, most importantly, to condition action in the world.

Clinical Strategies

I began with Dr. Charon describing her sense of the power of narrative in her practice, and we have also heard from Dr. Vannatta about how his engagement with Toni Morrison's *Beloved* allowed him to interact more fully with his patient. Before I set forth my sense of ways that the disciplinary understanding of the humanities can contribute to the education of physicians, let me turn to the clinical strategy another physician has developed in his practice. In *Pain and Suffering* I follow Dr. Scott Fishman in describing a 'functional' definition of pain. Rather than a 'subjective' definition of pain – for instance, a patient describing her pain as 'four' on a scale of zero to ten – or an essentialist definition of pain conceived in relation to a specific kind of sensory system, Fishman suggests that pain be understood in relation to life activities – in relation, although he does not say so, to narrative understanding. Thus, he argues that

> *the direct sensation associated with pain is not the only important variable and may not be the most important feature of the overall presentation of pain*. The real key to understanding pain and formulating an effective treatment plan is to look beyond the pain sensations to how those sensations are eroding a patient's quality of life. Specifically, how is the patient's pain affecting his or her *functioning* in daily life? (2012: 40)

Dr. Fishman suggests that we understand pain in terms of the functions it inhibits in order to create *objective pragmatic* goals that can organize *action in the world*. 'If, over the course of the day, [patients'] pain varies from a 4 to an 8 out of 10, I want to know what they can do when their pain is a 4 that they can't do when it is an 8. What meaningful activities are no longer possible and how were those activities lost over time? Once I can establish the level of functional losses in relation to pain, I can begin to envision possible goals for reclaiming lost functions' (2012: 32). The goals he envisions are *specific*: 'return to playing golf, ability to make love again, returning to gainful employment or volunteer work, driving a car, attending a child's sporting event, or leaving the reclining chair in the living room and sleeping in their beds at night' (2012: 32). In this, like Dr. Charon, he is pursuing the study of meaning and action together. Moreover, he is setting forth the systematic study of the practical reasoning of *phronesis* that Jerry and I pursue in our focus on the patient's *concern* in medicine.

The Humanities as a Discipline

Here, I should touch upon the nature and disciplines of the humanities, particularly in relation to schemas of experience. As I already noted, a recent encyclopedia description of the concept of 'schema' in cognitive science argues that schemas allow us 'to predict or infer unknown information in completely new situations' (Gureckis and Goldstone 2011: 725). I should add explicitly here – I have suggested this throughout this essay – that the goals of cognitive and experiential schemas are action in the world. Thus, in defining cognitive schemas, Thomas Nickles notes that 'schema theory denies that human perceptions and judgments consist in atomic events such as the passive ideas of the British associationists. Rather, our experiential inputs, and our output behaviors as well, are integrated into larger, active structures' (1998: 78). It is precisely this connection to action – the relationship between experience and action that is at the heart of Aristotle's notion of *phronesis* as *practical* reasoning – that makes the humanities so vital to medicine.

A catalogue of the disciplines of the humanities might make clear the ways in which the humanities study and engage with schemas of experience.

- **Literary studies** make the schemas that govern reading – particularly understood as the process of interpretation de Man mentions – and the schemas that govern the experience of reading both explicit and habitual.
- **History** makes the schemas that govern historical action and the schemas that govern our apprehensions and understandings of historical actions both explicit and habitual.
- **Art studies** make the schemas by which artworks are created and experienced explicit and habitual.
- **Philosophy** reflects upon schemas that organize and govern cognition, understanding, and experience.

As these descriptions suggest, each isolated humanities discipline participates in all of these actions: for that reason I can talk of the humanities as a single 'discipline.' Finally, the schemas the humanities study are *provisional*, which means: they constantly call for rethinking, reflection, and negotiation, like the negotiation between physician and patient in deciding what, finally, will count as 'health' – what will answer the 'chief concern' in any particular situation – in the life of an ailing person who is connected to the world in many different ways.

How the Humanities can help Train Doctors

As I have been suggesting, the humanities can help train doctors by systematically setting forth the schemas of experience – the experience of narrative, the experience of understanding (i.e., diagnosis), and the experience of interpersonal ethical behavior – in a way that is teachable as part of clinical training and practice for physicians. I conclude by returning to Dr. Kirch's description of the new MCAT for future medical students. In his letter I cite at the beginning of this essay, he mentions six particular areas that the new exam focuses on. I describe them here in three general categories of competency for medical practice.

I. The Need for Reasoning Skills

(1) Kirch notes explicitly the need for 'necessary reasoning skills to know where to seek answers[;] and

(2) how to solve problems in the clinical environment' in a world where medical

knowledge is so vast that no individual physician can be expected to fully command it all.

* * *

II. The Need for Cultural Competence

(3) He notes the MCAT's focus on the increase in the diversity of backgrounds in age, ethnicity, and other aspects of patients themselves (such as gender and class, though Kirch doesn't explicitly mention these aspects of diversity); and

(4) the concomitant need for knowledge in ethics, philosophy, cultural studies, sociology, psychology.

* * *

III. The Need for Strategies of Engagement and Deliberation

(5) He notes the exam's focus on the increase of chronic (as opposed to acute) medical conditions; and

(6) the need for teamwork and coordinated care among physicians, between physician and patient, and across a life-span of treatment.

As this listing suggests, Dr. Kirch's catalogue can be organized in relation to three problems facing medicine as a profession. I am arguing here (and we argue more fully in *The Chief Concern of Medicine*) that the humanities can offer systematic strategies for pursuing these ends. By way of conclusion, let me address each of these three areas, (I) the need for judicious decision-making in the face of the abundance of medical knowledge, (II) the need for cultural knowledge, and (III) the need for strategies of engaged action.

I: Judicious Decision-Making.

In his book, *The Checklist Manifesto*, Atul Gawande addresses Kirch's first problem, that of the enormous amount of biomedical knowledge available to physicians. He describes the fact that

> over the course of a year of office practice – which, by definition, excludes the patients seen in the hospital – physicians each evaluated an average of 250 different primary diseases and conditions. Their patients had more than nine hundred other active medical problems that had to be taken into account. The doctors each prescribed some three hundred medications, ordered more than a hundred different types of laboratory tests, and performed an average of forty different kinds of office procedures – from vaccinations to setting fractures.
> (2010: loc. 318)

The practical solution he suggests for this problem is the development of checklists, which are akin to – and sometimes actual examples of – the schemas I have been describing. In fact, at the end of *The Chief Concern of Medicine* Jerry and I present a series of checklists – growing out of engagement with the medical humanities – to help physicians habituate skills in listening to patients, in making diagnoses, and in pursuing ethical action in relation to their patients. Insofar as our checklists *habituate* practical reasoning and action in the clinic, they address the clinical environment as well.

II: The Need for Cultural Knowledge.

The second set of concerns addressed by the new MCAT is diversity, which focuses on the explosion of knowledge in relation to patients just as Gawande describes the explosion of knowledge on the level of practice. Diversity can be engaged through the kind of narrative deliberation – the suggested completion of her story – that Jerry exhibits with his patient with abdominal pain. Moreover, an awareness of narrative schemas can help healthcare workers be mindful of the significance of stories told by people of different backgrounds and with different assumptions about the world. And engagement with literary narrative provokes vicarious experience and empathetic understanding of what otherwise would be bewildering difference. But on a grittier, more practical level, the humanities can set forth *schemas of difference*, what we describe and set forth in our book as the systematic account of 'filters,' governed by emotion, culture, class, gender, age, that inflect the stories patients tell (2013: 196-210). Medical students, we have found, can be taught to be sensitive to such differences.

III: The Need for Engaged Action.

Finally, the advent of life-long rather than acute illness is a significant basis, I believe, of the new MCAT, in large part a measure of the success of medicine that, in solving many problems of acute disease has increased the occurrence of chronic disease. This necessitates the *deliberation* I have argued is an aspect of narrative engagement altogether, perhaps most apparent in the fact that patients and their physicians tell and retell stories. One of the most famous analyses of narrative is the German philosopher Walter Benjamin's essay 'The Storyteller.' In that essay he attempts to describe the power and importance of narrative, how it links generation to generation, builds community, and, in so doing, enacts the practical wisdom of *phronesis.* Benjamin describes the counsel that stories provide for their listeners, but at the same time he describes, in my judgment, the counsel that physicians offer to their patients. 'Counsel,' he says,

> is less an answer to a question than a proposal concerning the continuation of a story which is just unfolding. To seek this counsel one would first have to be able to tell the story. (Quite apart from the fact that a man is receptive to counsel only to the extent that he allows his situation to speak.) Counsel woven into the fabric of real life is wisdom. (1969: 86)

Such counseling, I believe, is the work of medicine in its aim of discovering with patients what might count as well-being in their particular circumstances and working to achieve that well-being in the patient. This is the practical wisdom that grows out of hard listening, strong attentiveness, and shared goals that can and should develop in the clinic. Such practical wisdom, I am arguing, is precisely what the humanities can bring to medical education and practice with great precision, efficiency, and explicit concern.

Bibliography

Benjamin, Walter, 'The Storyteller,' in *Illuminations*, trans. Harry Zohn. New York: Schocken Press, 1969.

Boyd, Brian, *On the Origin of Stories: Evolution, Cognition, and Fiction*. Cambridge, MA: Harvard University Press, 2009.

Gawande, Atul, *Better: A Surgeon's Notes on Performance*. New York: Metropolitan Books, 2007.

——, *The Checklist Manifesto: How to Get Things Right*. New York: Metropolitan Books, 2010. Amazon Kindle edition.

Gureckis, Todd and Robert Goldstone, 'Schema,' in *The Cambridge Encyclopedia of the Language Sciences*, ed. Patrick Colm Hogan. New York: Cambridge University Press, 2011, pp. 725-26.

Hardcastle, Valerie Gray, *The Myth of Pain*. Cambridge: MIT Press, 1999.

Hester, Casey and Ronald Schleifer, 'Enhancing Physician Empathy: Optimizing Learner Potential for Narrative Transportation,' *Enthymema* 16 (2016): 105-18.

Kirch, Darrell, 'MCAT 2015: An Open Letter to Pre-Med Students,' https://www.aamc.org/newsroom/reporter/march2012/276772/word.html.

Nickles, Thomas, 'Kuhn, Historical Philosophy of Science, and Case-Based Reasoning,' *Configurations* 6 (1998): 51-85.

Nussbaum, Martha, *Love's Knowledge: Essays on Philosophy and Literature*. New York: Oxford University Press, 1990.

Peirce, Charles Sanders, *Collected Papers*, vols. 1-6 edited by C. Hartshorne and P. Weiss; vols. 7-8 edited by A. Burks. Cambridge: Harvard University Press, 1931-1935, 1958.

Polkinghorne, Donald. *Narrative Knowing and the Human Sciences*. Albany: SUNY Press, 1988.

Schleifer, Ronald, *Intangible Materialism: The Body, Scientific Knowledge, and the Power of Language*. Minneapolis: University of Minnesota Press, 2009.

——, 'Modalities of Science: *Phronesis*, Narrative, and the Practices of Medicine,' *Danish Yearbook of Philosophy*, 44 (2009): 77-101.

——, *Pain and Suffering*. New York: Routledge, 2014.

——, 'The Semiotics of Sensation: A. J. Greimas and the Experience of Meaning,' *Semiotica* 214 (2017): 173-93.

——, *Political Economy of Modernism: Literature, Post-Classical Economics, and the Lower Middle Class*. Cambridge: Cambridge University Press, 2018.

Schleifer, Ronald and Jerry Vannatta, *The Chief Concern of Medicine: The Integration of the Medical Humanities and Narrative Knowledge into Medical Practices*. University of Michigan Press: Ann Arbor, 2013.

Steen, Francis, 'The Paradox of Narrative Thinking,' *Journal of Cultural and Evolutionary Psychology*, 3 (2005): 87-105.

Symons, Donald. *Rhesus Play*. Filmed and edited by John Melville Bishop; written and directed by Donald Symons. Harvard University Film Study Center: Cambridge, 1977.

Taylor, Charles, David Carr, and Paul Ricoeur, 'Discussion: Ricoeur on Narrative.' In *On Paul Ricoeur: Narrative and Interpretation*, ed. David Wood. New York: Routledge, 1991, pp. 160-188. Taylor's contribution appears on pp. 174-79.

Williams, William Carlos, *The Autobiography of William Carlos Williams*. New York: New Directions, 1951.

www.ingramcontent.com/pod-product-compliance
Ingram Content Group UK Ltd.
Pitfield, Milton Keynes, MK11 3LW, UK
UKHW020414250726
13967UKWH00007B/2642
9 780648 087885